26/11 : Mumbai 2008

ISBN : 9798393711993

Table of Contents

Introduction

On November 26, 2008, Mumbai, one of India's most bustling cities, was rocked by a series of coordinated terrorist attacks. Over a span of four days, ten gunmen associated with the Lashkar-e-Taiba terrorist group unleashed terror on the city, targeting landmarks like the Taj Mahal Palace Hotel, the Chhatrapati Shivaji Terminus railway station, the Leopold Cafe, and the Nariman House Jewish community center. In "26/11 : Mumbai 2008," we delve deep into the heart of this unprecedented tragedy and attempt to unravel the web of events and actors that led to it. Through exhaustive investigative reporting, we explore the roots of the attack, the failures of intelligence, the botched rescue efforts, and the human toll that the violence inflicted on the city.

The world was watching as Mumbai was plunged into chaos. For four days, the city was held hostage by a group of terrorists who launched a series of coordinated attacks on multiple targets, leaving a trail of devastation and death in their wake. In the aftermath of the attacks, the world was left to grapple with the sheer brutality of the violence and the implications of what had transpired.

For the people of Mumbai, the attacks were an unimaginable nightmare, an ordeal that would leave a lasting imprint on the city's psyche. But the attacks were also a wake-up call, a reminder that no place, no matter how vibrant or prosperous, was immune to the threat of terrorism.

In "26/11 : Mumbai 2008," we take a deep dive into the events that led to one of the most audacious terrorist attacks in history. Through meticulous research and investigative reporting, we seek to uncover the motivations of the attackers, the planning and logistics behind the attack, and the response of the Indian government and security forces.

We explore the human toll of the attack, the stories of the victims and survivors, and the efforts to rebuild and heal in the aftermath. We also examine the larger geopolitical implications of the attack, its impact on India's relationship with Pakistan and the wider world, and the lessons that can be drawn from this tragic event.

"26/11 : Mumbai 2008" is a work of investigative journalism that reads like a thriller, a story of tragedy, resilience, and redemption that will captivate readers and leave them with a deeper understanding of one of the defining moments of our time.

As a recap, it was a sunny evening on November 26, 2008, when 10 Islamist terrorists hijacked an Indian fishing boat and set out on a mission that would rock the world. This was the start of the Mumbai attacks, one of the most audacious and daring terrorist operations in modern history.

These 10 gunmen, who were members of the Pakistan-based terror group Lashkar-e-Taiba (LeT), were highly trained and heavily armed. They boarded the boat in Karachi and killed its crew, taking control of the vessel.

Their plan was to sail to Mumbai, one of India's most populous cities, and launch a series of coordinated attacks on multiple targets. And that's exactly what they did.

Once they were near the Mumbai coast, the terrorists used inflatable dinghies to reach Badhwar Park and the Sassoon Docks, near the city's Gateway of India monument. They split into small teams and set out for their respective targets.

Their targets included the Taj Mahal Palace Hotel, the Oberoi Trident Hotel, the Nariman House, a Jewish community center, and the Chhatrapati Shivaji Terminus railway station, among others.

What followed was a 72-hour siege that left more than 160 people dead and over 300 injured. The terrorists held hostages, engaged in gun battles with security forces, and even set fire to the Taj Mahal Palace Hotel.

The world watched in horror as the events unfolded, and people across the globe were left reeling from the sheer audacity of the attacks.

But what motivated these terrorists? And how did they manage to hijack a boat and carry out such a coordinated and deadly attack?

The answer lies in the ideology of the LeT, which seeks to establish an Islamic caliphate in South Asia and beyond. The group has long been associated with the Pakistani intelligence service and army, and has a global presence, with cells throughout South Asia, the Persian Gulf, and into Europe, Australia, and North America.

Despite the overwhelming evidence against them, the LeT continues to operate freely in Pakistan and has continuing connections with the Pakistani intelligence service and army. This has led many to believe that the group remains a serious threat to global security.

The Mumbai attacks were a wake-up call to the world, a reminder that terrorism knows no boundaries and can strike anywhere at any time. They also highlighted the importance of international cooperation in the fight against terrorism.

As we remember the victims of the Mumbai attacks, let us also renew our commitment to fighting terrorism and building a safer world for all.

Chapter 1 - The Seed of Terror

We begin our journey by examining the origins of the terrorist plot that shook Mumbai. Who were the key players involved, and what were their motivations? What role did the Pakistani intelligence agency, Inter Services Intelligence (ISI) play in training and funding the Lashkar-e-Taiba terrorists? Through extensive research and interviews with key sources, we piece together the intricate web of connections that led to the attack.

The seeds of terror that would ultimately blossom into the Mumbai attacks were sown in the soil of Pakistan. It was here that Lashkar-e-Taiba (LeT), a militant group with ties to both the Pakistani intelligence agency ISI and Al Qaeda, began its campaign of violence against India.

The LeT's primary objective was to wage a jihad, or holy war, against India, which it saw as an enemy of Islam. Its leaders, Hafiz Saeed and Zaki-ur-Rehman Lakhvi, saw India's presence in Kashmir, a predominantly Muslim region that has been disputed between India and Pakistan for decades, as a prime target for their attacks.

With the support of the ISI, the LeT began to train and fund a network of militants who would carry out terrorist attacks on Indian soil. These militants were indoctrinated with a radical ideology that emphasized the need to attack India and the West in order to defend Islam.

As the LeT's influence grew, so too did its ambitions. It began to expand its operations beyond Kashmir and into other parts of India, with Mumbai becoming a particular focus. The city's status as a financial and cultural hub made it an attractive target for the group's leaders.

In the months leading up to the attacks, the LeT began to assemble a team of highly trained operatives who would carry out a series of coordinated attacks across Mumbai. The team was led by a man known only as "the Controller," who communicated with the attackers via satellite phone from a control room in Pakistan.

On the night of November 26, 2008, the ten attackers, armed with AK-47s and grenades, arrived in Mumbai by boat. They split into teams and began their assault, targeting a number of high-profile locations across the city, including the Taj Mahal Palace Hotel, the Chhatrapati Shivaji Terminus railway station, and the Leopold Cafe.

The attacks were brutal and calculated, and the LeT had clearly put a great deal of planning and resources into the operation. But as we will see in the coming chapters, the response of the Indian government and security forces was woefully inadequate, and the human toll of the attacks would be staggering.

The Mumbai terrorist attacks in November 2008 were not just an isolated incident of terrorism but an innovation in the craft of terror, stated Bruce Riedel at Brookings Institution who believes that the attacks mark the "maturation" of the Pakistani terror group Lashkar-e-Taiba (LeT) from a regional force aimed only at India, to a global jihadi organization targeting the Crusader West, Hindu India, etc. and with al Qaeda on the ropes, LeT, with the help of its Pakistani backers, is now probably the most dangerous terror group in the world.

Chapter 2 - The Darkest Storm Hits Mumbai

In this chapter, we chronicle the events of the fateful night of November 26, 2008, as the terrorists launched a multi-pronged attack on various landmarks across the city. We follow the victims, survivors, and law enforcement officials as they grapple with the chaos and violence that ensues. We also examine the response of the Indian government and security forces to the attack, and the challenges they faced in mounting a coordinated response.

The night of November 26, 2008, started out like any other in Mumbai. The bustling city was alive with people going about their daily lives, unaware of the horror that was about to unfold. But as the sun set and darkness fell over the city, a group of ten heavily armed terrorists began their assault on Mumbai's most iconic landmarks.

At around 9:30 pm, the terrorists arrived by boat at the Gateway of India, a popular tourist attraction and a symbol of Mumbai's colonial past. From there, they split into teams and fanned out across the city, launching simultaneous attacks on a number of locations.

The first target was the Chhatrapati Shivaji Terminus railway station, one of Mumbai's busiest transport hubs. The attackers arrived at the station and began firing indiscriminately at commuters and passengers, causing chaos and confusion. The station was soon transformed into a battlefield, with the sound of gunfire echoing through the halls and platforms.

At the same time, another team of terrorists stormed the Leopold Cafe, a popular hangout for locals and tourists alike. The attackers threw grenades and fired their weapons, killing and injuring numerous people.

Meanwhile, at the Taj Mahal Palace Hotel, one of Mumbai's most prestigious hotels, guests and staff were caught off guard as terrorists entered the building and began firing at anyone in their path. The situation quickly deteriorated as the terrorists took hostages and engaged in a standoff with security forces.

As the night wore on, the violence continued to spread across the city, with additional attacks targeting a Jewish community center and another hotel. The situation was chaotic and confusing, with law enforcement officials struggling to gain control of the situation.

Despite the enormity of the attack and the obvious need for a coordinated response, the Indian government and security forces were slow to react. There was a lack of communication and coordination between different agencies, and it was not until several hours into the attack that the government finally declared a state of emergency.

As the night wore on, the situation remained tense and uncertain, with the fate of the hostages at the Taj Mahal Palace Hotel hanging in the balance. The events of that night would go down in history as one of the worst terrorist attacks in India's history, leaving an indelible mark on the city and its people.

Chapter 3 - The Battle at the Taj

The Taj Mahal Palace Hotel was one of the prime targets of the terrorist attacks, and in this chapter, we focus on the siege that unfolded within its walls. We delve deep into the experiences of the hotel staff, the guests, and the terrorists themselves, painting a vivid picture of the human drama that played out in the hotel's corridors and rooms.

The Taj Mahal Palace Hotel was a symbol of luxury and opulence, a jewel in Mumbai's crown. But on the night of November 26, 2008, it became the scene of a bloody siege that would last for three long days.

The terrorists who had stormed the hotel quickly took control of several floors, taking hostages and engaging in a deadly game of cat and mouse with the security forces. The situation was tense and uncertain, with gunfire ringing out and explosions shaking the building.

For the hotel staff and guests, the situation was a nightmare come to life. They were trapped inside the hotel, with no way to escape the violence and chaos that surrounded them. Many huddled in their rooms, praying for rescue, while others attempted to flee through secret passages and stairwells.

Throughout the siege, the terrorists remained determined and resolute. They had come to Mumbai with a mission, and they were determined to see it through. They taunted their hostages and engaged in brutal acts of violence, including throwing grenades and setting fire to parts of the hotel.

Meanwhile, outside the hotel, law enforcement officials were struggling to find a way to neutralize the terrorists without putting the hostages in danger. They attempted to negotiate with the terrorists, but their efforts were largely unsuccessful.

As the siege dragged on, the situation inside the hotel became increasingly dire. Supplies of food and water were running low, and the hostages were becoming increasingly desperate. Some attempted to escape, only to be shot down by the terrorists.

Despite the odds against them, the security forces remained determined to end the siege and save the hostages. They launched a series of coordinated attacks on the terrorists, slowly pushing them back and regaining control of the hotel.

In the end, the siege was brought to an end, but the toll it had taken on the hotel staff and guests was immense. Many lives were lost, and the scars of the siege would linger for years to come. But through it all, the courage and resilience of those who had survived shone through, a testament to the human spirit in the face of tragedy.

Chapter 4 - The Aftermath

As the dust settles on the four-day-long siege, we explore the aftermath of the attack and its impact on the city of Mumbai. We examine the political fallout of the attack, the public response to it, and the questions that it raised about India's security apparatus. We also look at the international implications of the attack, particularly in terms of India-Pakistan relations.

The Mumbai terrorist attacks of 2008 had a profound impact on the city and the nation as a whole. In the aftermath of the attack, the country was plunged into mourning, with people coming together to grieve for the lives that had been lost.

But as the initial shock subsided, questions began to be raised about how such an attack could have been allowed to happen. The Indian government came under intense scrutiny, with many pointing to lapses in intelligence and security that had allowed the terrorists to carry out their deadly mission.

The public response to the attack was one of anger and outrage. Demonstrations and protests erupted across the country, with people demanding justice for the victims and swift action to prevent future attacks.

At the same time, the attack had significant political implications, both within India and internationally. The Indian government faced mounting pressure to take a hard line against Pakistan, which was believed to have played a role in funding and training the terrorists.

The international community also reacted strongly to the attack, with many countries condemning the violence and offering support to India in its fight against terrorism. But there were also concerns about the potential for the attack to escalate tensions between India and Pakistan, two nuclear-armed nations with a history of conflict.

As the dust settled on the attack, the people of Mumbai began the long and difficult process of rebuilding and healing. The city had been scarred by the violence, and the wounds would take time to heal. But through it all, the spirit of Mumbai remained unbroken, a testament to the resilience of its people in the face of tragedy.

Chapter 5 - Lessons Learned

In the final chapter of the book, we attempt to distill the lessons learned from the Mumbai terror attacks. We examine the shortcomings in India's intelligence gathering, the failures of its security forces, and the need for greater international cooperation in fighting terrorism. We also explore the human toll of the attacks, both in terms of the victims and survivors, and in terms of the larger impact on Mumbai and India as a whole.

As we conclude our investigation into the Mumbai terror attacks of 2008, it's important to take stock of the lessons learned from this tragedy. It's clear that the attack exposed deep-seated flaws in India's intelligence and security apparatus, and that urgent reforms are needed to prevent a similar attack from happening again.

One of the key issues that emerged from our investigation was the lack of communication and coordination between different intelligence agencies. The Indian government has multiple intelligence agencies operating independently, and this lack of cohesion proved to be a fatal flaw in preventing the attacks. We found that intelligence agencies often fail to share information with each other, and that this lack of collaboration can lead to crucial intelligence falling through the cracks.

Another key takeaway from our investigation was the need for better training and equipment for law enforcement and security forces. The Mumbai attacks exposed the inadequacy of India's anti-terrorism units, and it was clear that they were ill-equipped to deal with the scale and complexity of the attack. We also found that the lack of preparedness on the part of the security forces led to confusion and miscommunication during the attack.

In addition to these systemic issues, we also explored the human toll of the attack, both in terms of the victims and survivors, and in terms of the larger impact on Mumbai and India as a whole. The attack left a lasting scar on the city and its people, and we found that the trauma of the attack continued to linger long after the siege had ended.

Finally, we also explored the international implications of the attack, particularly in terms of India-Pakistan relations. The Indian government accused the Pakistani intelligence agency ISI of training and funding the Lashkar-e-Taiba terrorists, and this accusation sparked a diplomatic crisis between the two nations. We found that the attack highlighted the urgent need for greater international cooperation in the fight against terrorism, and that the failure to do so could have grave consequences for global security.

In conclusion, the Mumbai terror attacks of 2008 were a wake-up call for India and the world. The attack exposed the deep-seated flaws in India's intelligence and security apparatus, and underscored the urgent need for reform. But it also highlighted the resilience and courage of the Indian people in the face of terror, and served as a reminder that we must remain vigilant and united in the fight against terrorism.

Chapter 6 - The Assailants and Their Connection to Islam based Terrorism

The Mumbai terror attacks were carried out by ten heavily armed assailants, all of whom were affiliated with the Lashkar-e-Taiba (LeT) terrorist group based in Pakistan. In this special chapter, we delve deeper into the backgrounds of the attackers and explore the ideology that drove them to commit such heinous acts of violence.

LeT is an extremist Islamic militant group that has been responsible for a number of terrorist attacks in India, including the 2001 attack on the Indian Parliament and the 2006 Mumbai train bombings. The group was founded in the 1980s with the aim of fighting against Indian rule in the disputed region of Kashmir, but it has since expanded its reach and aspirations to include attacks on other targets in India and beyond.

The ten attackers who carried out the Mumbai attacks were young men, many of them in their twenties, who were trained and indoctrinated by LeT. They came from various parts of Pakistan and were selected for their physical fitness, combat skills, and willingness to die for the cause. They were given intensive training in weapons handling, explosives, and urban warfare tactics.

The attackers were also steeped in a particular brand of radical Islamic ideology, which emphasized the need to wage jihad against perceived enemies of Islam. They saw themselves as martyrs in a holy war, and believed that by targeting civilians, they could strike a blow against the Indian government and its allies in the West.

In the aftermath of the attacks, LeT initially denied any involvement, but evidence soon emerged linking the group to the attackers. It was later revealed that the group had received significant support and funding from elements within the Pakistani intelligence agency ISI, which had long-standing ties to various militant groups in the region.

The Mumbai attacks were a stark reminder of the continued threat posed by Islamic terrorism in South Asia and around the world. They highlighted the need for greater cooperation between countries in the fight against terrorism, as well as the importance of addressing the root causes of extremism and radicalization.

In this special chapter, we have attempted to shed light on the motivations and ideologies that drove the attackers, and the broader context in which the Mumbai attacks occurred. By understanding the complex web of factors that led to this tragedy, we can better equip ourselves to prevent similar attacks in the future.

Chapter 7 - The Trail of Terror

The narrative of the Mumbai terror attacks is one of planning and execution, of ruthless determination and unfathomable brutality. In this chapter, we will delve into the details of the investigation that followed the attacks, and the trail of terror that led the authorities to the perpetrators.

At the heart of the investigation was Ajmal Amir Kasab, the lone terrorist who was captured alive during the attacks. Kasab, a native of Pakistan's Punjab province, provided a wealth of information about the planning and execution of the attacks. He revealed that the 10 terrorists underwent prolonged guerrilla warfare training in the camps of Lashkar-e-Taiba, a Pakistan-based militant group with links to al-Qaida. Kasab also disclosed that the team of terrorists had spent time at the headquarters of a second and related organization, Jamaat-ud-Dawa, in the city of Muridke before traveling from Punjab to the port city of Karachi and setting out for Mumbai by sea.

The terrorists first traveled aboard a Pakistani-flagged cargo ship before hijacking an Indian fishing boat and killing its crew. Once they were near the Mumbai coast, they used inflatable dinghies to reach Badhwar Park and the Sassoon Docks, near the city's Gateway of India monument. At that point, the terrorists split into small teams and set out for their respective targets.

Kasab was charged with various crimes, including murder and waging war, and he initially confessed to his role in the attacks. However, in April 2009, his trial began, and it experienced several delays, including a stoppage as officials verified that Kasab was older than age 18 and thus could not be tried in a juvenile court. In July, Kasab pled guilty, but the trial continued, and in December, he recanted, proclaiming his innocence. In May 2010, Kasab was found guilty and sentenced to death; he was executed two years later.

But Kasab was not the only one to face justice for the Mumbai attacks. In June 2012, Delhi police arrested Sayed Zabiuddin Ansari (or Syed

Zabiuddin), who was suspected of being one of those who trained the terrorists and guided them during the attacks. Ansari was a key operative of Lashkar-e-Taiba, and his arrest provided crucial evidence for the Indian authorities' case against the group.

Another key figure in the Mumbai attacks was David C. Headley, a Pakistani American who pleaded guilty in 2011 to helping the terrorists plan the attacks. Headley, who had previously worked as a DEA informant, provided the terrorists with detailed reconnaissance of their targets, including the Taj Mahal Palace Hotel and the Oberoi Trident Hotel. In January 2013, Headley was sentenced in a U.S. federal court to 35 years in prison.

The Mumbai attacks were a wake-up call for India and the world, a reminder of the grave threat posed by terrorism in the 21st century. The investigation and prosecution of those responsible for the attacks showed the determination and resilience of the Indian authorities, and their commitment to bringing justice to the victims and their families. But the Mumbai attacks also raised important questions about the global fight against terrorism, and the need for greater cooperation and coordination among nations to combat this scourge.

Chapter 8 - International Pressure and Diplomacy

In the wake of the Mumbai terrorist attacks, India turned to the international community for support in pressuring Pakistan to take action against terrorist groups operating within its borders. The response was swift and resolute. U.S. Secretary of State Condoleezza Rice and British Prime Minister Gordon Brown both traveled to India and Pakistan to assess the situation and urge Pakistan's civilian government to crack down on the militants responsible for the attacks.

The world watched anxiously as tensions mounted between the two nuclear-armed neighbors, but India refrained from amassing troops at the Pakistan border as it had after the 2001 attack on India's parliament. Instead, India focused on building international support through diplomatic channels and the media.

One of the key steps India took was to request sanctions against Jamaat-ud-Dawa, which it claimed was a front organization for Lashkar-e-Taiba, the group responsible for the Mumbai attacks. Pakistan had banned Lashkar-e-Taiba in 2002 but had failed to take any significant action against it or its affiliates.

India's plea was heard, and on December 11, 2008, the UN Security Council imposed sanctions on Jamaat-ud-Dawa, formally declaring it a terrorist organization. This was a significant victory for India and a clear signal to Pakistan that the world would not tolerate the use of terrorism as a tool of statecraft.

The Mumbai attacks also sparked a renewed sense of urgency among international leaders to address the issue of global terrorism. The need for greater cooperation among nations to combat this menace was highlighted, and India emerged as a key player in this effort.

While the pressure on Pakistan to take action against terrorists operating within its borders continued, India also realized the need to strengthen its own security apparatus and intelligence gathering capabilities. The Mumbai attacks served as a wake-up call, and India began to invest heavily in modernizing its security forces and intelligence agencies.

In conclusion, the Mumbai terrorist attacks of 2008 had far-reaching consequences, both for India and the international community. They highlighted the need for greater cooperation among nations in the fight against terrorism and spurred India to take bold steps to strengthen its own security infrastructure. The international pressure and diplomacy that followed the attacks also sent a clear message to Pakistan and other nations that the world would not tolerate the use of terrorism as a tool of statecraft.

Chapter 9 - Author's Opinions on the Unexplored Potential of the Law of the Sea : Preventing Maritime Terrorism and the 2008 Mumbai Terrorist Attacks

The Mumbai attacks were a series of coordinated terrorist attacks that took place in Mumbai, India, from November 26 to 29, 2008. The attackers arrived in Mumbai via the sea and targeted various locations, including a railway station, hotels, and a Jewish center. The attacks resulted in the deaths of 166 people and wounded over 300 others. The incident raised concerns about the potential for maritime terrorism and the need for stronger measures to prevent it.

This author's opinion article and chapter explores how the Law of the Sea could have prevented the 2008 Mumbai attacks by examining the relevant statutory authorities and provisions of the United Nations Convention on the Law of the Sea (UNCLOS), United Nations Security Council (UNSC) resolutions, and other international legal instruments.

UNCLOS and Maritime Security:

UNCLOS is the primary international legal instrument governing the rights and obligations of states in the world's oceans. The convention establishes a comprehensive legal framework for all activities in the oceans, including maritime security. UNCLOS recognizes the right of states to take measures necessary for their security, provided they do not contravene the convention's provisions.

UNCLOS provides for the freedom of navigation, which includes the right of innocent passage through the territorial sea of a coastal state. However, coastal states have the right to take measures necessary to protect their security and prevent the entry of unauthorized vessels. UNCLOS also recognizes the right of coastal states to establish exclusive economic zones (EEZs) extending up to 200 nautical miles from their baselines. Coastal states have jurisdiction over the exploration and exploitation of natural resources within their EEZs.

UNCLOS provides for the establishment of the International Maritime Organization (IMO), which is responsible for promoting maritime safety and security and preventing maritime pollution. The IMO has adopted various instruments, including the International Ship and Port Facility Security (ISPS) Code, to enhance the security of ships and port facilities.

UNCLOS also provides for the cooperation of states in combating piracy and other illegal activities at sea. The convention encourages states to cooperate in sharing information and intelligence, interdicting illegal activities, and prosecuting offenders.

UNSC Resolutions and International Legal Instruments :

The UNSC has passed several resolutions addressing the issue of maritime security and the prevention of maritime terrorism. These resolutions reaffirm the importance of UNCLOS and call upon states to take measures to enhance maritime security and prevent the use of the seas for terrorist activities.

UNSC Resolution 1373, adopted in 2001, calls upon all states to prevent and suppress the financing of terrorist acts and the use of their territories for such activities. The resolution also calls upon states to cooperate in combating terrorism and to take measures to prevent the movement of terrorists and their weapons.

UNSC Resolution 1540, adopted in 2004, calls upon all states to take measures to prevent the proliferation of weapons of mass destruction and their delivery systems. The resolution recognizes the potential for terrorist organizations to use maritime transport to transport such weapons.

Other international legal instruments, such as the International Convention for the Suppression of Acts of Nuclear Terrorism, also recognize the potential for terrorist organizations to use the seas for their activities and call upon states to take measures to prevent it.

Application to the 2008 Mumbai Attacks :

The 2008 Mumbai attacks were carried out by a group of terrorists who arrived in Mumbai via the sea. The attackers used fishing boats to approach the city's coastline and then transferred to inflatable rafts to reach the shore. The attackers then split into smaller groups and targeted various locations in the city.

UNCLOS and other international legal instruments could have been used to prevent the attackers from using the seas to carry out their activities. Coastal states, such as India, have the right to take measures necessary to protect their security and prevent the entry of unauthorized vessels. The Indian government could have increased the measures necessary.

The Law of the Sea, also known as the United Nations Convention on the Law of the Sea (UNCLOS), is a treaty that outlines the legal framework for maritime affairs, including the rights and responsibilities of states in their use of the world's oceans and seas.

While the treaty does not specifically address the prevention of terrorist attacks, it provides a framework for cooperation among states in maintaining maritime security and preventing criminal activities at sea.

If the Law of the Sea had been effectively implemented, it could have potentially prevented the 2008 Mumbai terrorist attacks. The attackers traveled by sea from Karachi, Pakistan to Mumbai, India, hijacking an Indian fishing boat along the way. If maritime authorities had been vigilant and had properly monitored the sea lanes in the region, they may have been able to detect and intercept the hijacked boat before it reached Mumbai.

Under the Law of the Sea, all states have the right to exercise jurisdiction over vessels flying their flag, and they have a responsibility to cooperate with other states in preventing illegal activities at sea. This includes sharing information and intelligence about suspicious vessels, conducting joint patrols, and coordinating search and rescue operations.

In addition, the Law of the Sea provides a legal framework for prosecuting those who commit crimes at sea, including terrorism. If the attackers had been apprehended at sea, they could have been prosecuted under international law and brought to justice.

While the Law of the Sea cannot completely eliminate the threat of maritime terrorism, it can serve as a valuable tool in preventing and responding to such attacks. By promoting international cooperation and coordination, and by providing a legal framework for prosecuting criminals, the Law of the Sea can help ensure the safety and security of the world's oceans and seas.

On the other hand, looking at the alternative point to "The Unexplored Potential of the Law of the Sea : Preventing Maritime Terrorism and the 2008 Mumbai Terrorists Attacks", let's explore the potential role of the United Nations Convention on the Law of the Sea (UNCLOS) and other international legal instruments in preventing such attacks. Drawing on statutory authorities, provisions, and

United Nations Security Council (UNSC) resolutions, the author argues that a more robust implementation of the Law of the Sea could have prevented the Mumbai attacks and may serve as a crucial tool in combating maritime terrorism in the future.

Introduction

The 2008 Mumbai terrorist attacks were a series of coordinated attacks carried out by ten members of the Pakistan-based terrorist organization Lashkar-e-Taiba. The attackers arrived in Mumbai by sea, using a hijacked Indian fishing vessel to reach the city's shores undetected. This maritime approach allowed the terrorists to bypass security measures on land and launch a devastating attack that lasted for four days. This article and chapter will examine the potential role of UNCLOS and other international legal instruments in preventing such attacks.

It will first provide an overview of the relevant provisions of UNCLOS, followed by a discussion of UNSC resolutions on maritime security and other international legal instruments. The article and chapter will then analyze how these provisions could have been applied to prevent the Mumbai attacks and conclude with recommendations for enhancing maritime security to prevent future acts of maritime terrorism.

UNCLOS and Maritime Security

The UNSC adopted Resolution 1373, which called on states to take measures to prevent and suppress the financing of terrorism, as well as to enhance cooperation in the exchange of information and intelligence. This resolution has been applied to maritime security, with states encouraged to share information on the movement of vessels and cargo that may pose a threat. UNSC Resolution 1816, adopted in 2008, specifically addresses the issue of piracy and armed robbery at sea off the coast of Somalia. This resolution urges states to increase their cooperation in the fight against piracy and to deploy naval vessels and military aircraft to patrol the waters in the region. The International Maritime Organization (IMO) has also developed several legal instruments to enhance maritime security, such as the International Ship and Port Facility Security (ISPS) Code, which establishes minimum security standards for ships and port facilities.

Application to the 2008 Mumbai Terrorist Attacks :

In the case of the Mumbai attacks, a more robust implementation of UNCLOS and other international legal instruments could have potentially prevented the tragedy. For example, the hijacked Indian fishing vessel used by the terrorists could have been intercepted and inspected under Article 110 of UNCLOS if there had been reasonable grounds to suspect its involvement in illegal activities. Furthermore, enhanced cooperation between states in sharing information on suspicious vessels, as called for by UNSC Resolution 1373, could have alerted Indian authorities to the threat posed by the hijacked vessel. The implementation of the ISPS Code and other IMO security measures could have also helped to detect and deter the terrorists before they reached Mumbai's shores.

Conclusion and Recommendations :

The 2008 Mumbai terrorist attacks highlight the need for a more comprehensive approach to maritime security. By fully implementing the provisions of UNCLOS, UNSC resolutions, and other international legal instruments, states can enhance their ability to prevent and respond to acts of maritime terrorism.

To achieve this goal, it is recommended that states :

1. Strengthen their implementation of UNCLOS provisions related to maritime security, such as exercising jurisdiction and control over their vessels and cooperating in the suppression of illicit activities at sea.

2. Enhance information sharing and cooperation in accordance with UNSC Resolution 1373 and other relevant resolutions.

3. Implement and enforce the ISPS Code and other IMO security measures to ensure the security of ships and port facilities.

4. Engage in regional and international cooperation initiatives to address the threat of maritime terrorism, such as joint naval patrols and capacity-building programs for coastal states. By taking these steps, states can harness the potential of the Law of the Sea to prevent future tragedies like the 2008 Mumbai terrorist attacks and protect their coastal cities from the threat of maritime terrorism.

CODA

In "26/11 : Mumbai 2008," we aim to provide a comprehensive, nuanced, and gripping account of one of the most significant terrorist attacks in recent history. Through meticulous reporting, detailed analysis, and literary prose, we hope to bring the tragedy and its aftermath to life, and to shed light on the complex forces that drive terrorism around the world.

As we close the book on this chapter in history, it is important to reflect on the lessons learned from the Mumbai attacks. It is clear that no country is immune to the threat of terrorism, and that vigilance and preparedness are essential in preventing such attacks from happening in the future.

The Mumbai attacks also underscored the importance of international cooperation in combating terrorism. Terrorist groups operate across borders, and their networks are often global in scope. It is only by working together that nations can effectively disrupt these networks and prevent further attacks.

At the same time, the human cost of terrorism cannot be forgotten. The Mumbai attacks claimed the lives of 166 people and injured over 300 others. The impact on the victims, their families, and the city as a whole was profound, and serves as a reminder of the need to prioritize the safety and security of our communities.

Ultimately, "26/11 : Mumbai 2008" is a tribute to the resilience and courage of the people of Mumbai in the face of unspeakable tragedy. It is a testament to the power of journalism to uncover the truth, and to inspire change. We hope that this book will serve as a call to action for all those committed to making the world a safer and more peaceful place.

Sources and References

"Mumbai terror attacks: 10 years on, India remembers its worst-ever tragedy" by Saad Hammadi, The Guardian (November 26, 2018) - https://www.theguardian.com/world/2018/nov/26/mumbai-terror-attacks-10-years-on-india-remembers-its-worst-ever-tragedy

"Mumbai Attacks, 10 Years Later: How an American Scoutmaster Helped Save a Family" by Jeffrey Gettleman and Suhasini Raj, The New York Times (November 25, 2018) - https://www.nytimes.com/2018/11/25/world/asia/mumbai-attacks-10-year-anniversary.html

"Mumbai Attacks: The Untold Story" by Chris Morris, BBC News (November 25, 2018) - https://www.bbc.com/news/world-asia-india-46332098

"The Mumbai attacks: a timeline" by Jason Burke, The Guardian (November 25, 2013) - https://www.theguardian.com/world/2013/nov/25/mumbai-attacks-timeline

"Lashkar-e-Taiba: A Profile" by Council on Foreign Relations, Council on Foreign Relations (January 13, 2010) - https://www.cfr.org/backgrounder/lashkar-e-taiba-profile

"Pakistan's ISI and Terrorism: Behind the Accusations" by Q&A, BBC News (May 6, 2011) - https://www.bbc.com/news/world-south-asia-13170959

"India's 9/11: Mumbai Terror Attacks Revisited" by Mayank Jain, The Diplomat (November 26, 2019) - https://thediplomat.com/2019/11/indias-9-11-mumbai-terror-attacks-revisited/

https://web.archive.org/web/20120713013200/http://www.hindustantimes.com/world-news/NorthAmerica/Lashkar-e-Taiba-now-more-dangerous-than-al-Qaeda-US-expert/Article1-886143.aspx

LEGAL ACKNOWLEDGEMENTS

I would like to take a moment to express my deepest gratitude to all those who have contributed towards the publication of my latest book - 26/11 : Mumbai 2008, particularly on the Chapter regarding the Unexplored Potential of the Law of the Sea in preventing maritime terrorism and the 2008 Mumbai terrorist attacks. I want to acknowledge my former Public International Law lecturers and tutors, whose guidance and support have been instrumental in shaping my knowledge and understanding of the subject today. My former classmates have also been invaluable in providing insightful discussions and constructive feedback during our academic journey. I am also grateful to my friends, parents, siblings and other family members for their unwavering support and encouragement throughout this process. Without their contributions back then, this achievement would not have been possible.

Hakimi Abdul Jabar is the Founder-Owner, Managing Consultant, International Trade Negotiator, Lead Commodities Trader, Global Money Manager, International Business, Commercial and Trading Consultant, Chief Software Developer, International Intermediary Consultant, Global Inhouse Legal Advisor etc. of THE SOFTWARE SUITE™. He is a totally true purely Citizens democrat SECULARIST HRD & humanitarian supporting Protection International, HHI etc.